Marilyn –

JENIFER JOY MADDEN

Stay durable!
Best,
Jeni

Copyright © 2013, 2014 by Jenifer Joy Madden
Version 1.3

All rights reserved. No portion of this book may be reproduced in any form by any means without express permission, including reprints, photocopying, recording, or any future means of reproducing text. Brief excerpts may be used with attribution.

ISBN: 1492750174

Cover and Interior Design: Patty Wallace, MonkeyPAWcreative.com
Editor: Michele Matrisciani, Bookchic.net
Copy Editor: Nicole Joy Hales

Published in the United States by:

Durable Human Productions
P.O. Box 292
Dunn Loring, VA 22027

Inquiries: info@durablehuman.com

Dedicated to my mother, Esther Fischle Joy

My life is changing, and not for the better.

Courtesy of Christine Zenino, Wikimedia commons

It used to be when I opened my eyes in the morning, my mind wandered through traces of a dream or thoughts of the coming day. But now when I wake up, I only have one thing in mind: checking my cellphone. Later, when I'm supposed to be working, an hour goes *poof!* as I slip down another rabbit hole of a link on Twitter.

My dog's hold-it power has doubled in all the times she's waited for me to read *one more email.* The other day, as my daughter was confiding in me about her love life, she almost burst into tears when she caught me glancing at my laptop instead of at her.

My life is changing, and not for the better. A strange callousness has crept into my most cherished relationships. While once I gave my teenage son a quick neck massage if he stopped to chat, these days I sit back and half-listen as I thumb through my email.

I feel like the Greenland ice sheet — important parts of me are just melting away.

We all share the malaise. If you need a shoulder to cry on, social media doesn't cut it. When you actually try to call people, they don't pick up the phone. If you meet your sister and her son for a rare lunch, he spends the entire meal texting.

It's like when you play ball in the ocean on a windy day. Until you stop to look around, you don't realize you've been

swept down shore. That's what's happening to us humans. As a species, we are drifting from our usual sources of sustenance, strength, and solace. We've been blown off course from self-reliance, genuine relationships, and any semblance of down time. Wrestling with a fire hose of information, we've been knocked out of the natural rhythms that have always guided us. Although we're wired to take our cues from sunlight, the only windows some of us see are made by Microsoft.

It has a lot to do with the way we spend our time.

Before the digital age, 24 hours just felt longer.

Especially as kids, we seemed to have endless hours to chase down whatever random idea popped into our heads. Acting on our innate curiosity, we learned not only about the world around us, but also the environment of our own minds. We had time to get to know ourselves, what interested us and what we did best. We each developed in our own way, so as grownups we contributed many different talents and ideas. Consequently, each person brought a different skill set to society which, knit together, created a vibrant economy.

Foo Fighters founder Dave Grohl remembers the countless hours he spent switching between cassette decks so he could record himself playing drums and guitar in the same song. He was driven by his inner grit and creativity, as he proudly proclaims, "I had done all of this by myself."

In the summers when Steve Wozniak was growing up in the California suburbs, he and his friends had nothing much to do, but that didn't mean they were doing nothing.

One time, Woz snatched some wire off a telephone repair truck. He and his buddies used it to rig up an intercom between their houses that they actually got to work.

By today's standards, because he had so few scheduled activities, Woz's childhood might be considered boring or unproductive (ironic as that is). But, considering his lifetime of accomplishments, we see that *boredom demands a solution.* With nothing in particular to entertain them, Woz and his friends amused *themselves.*

Because he had time, Woz followed his curiosity and discovered he was good at making things. In college, he made friends with a high school kid who also liked to build stuff. His last name was Jobs. Not long after, they pooled their time and created the world's first personal computer.

One wonders what might have happened if the Steves were born today. Would the flicker of a parent's smartphone usurp young Jobs' wandering thoughts? Would video games devour little Woz's time to tinker?

Back before cellphones (BC), there was no alternative but to rely on yourself to solve problems. I remember one winter day—the snow must have been a foot deep. I was playing with my neighbor in the woods, when I tripped on a root and slipped all the way down a steep gully. Though it took a couple of hours, my pal patiently waited as I slowly clambered out. We got home just as night was falling, but I never said a thing to my mom. It was no big deal—just something that happened when you were outside.

You can probably think of a time as a kid when you were in a tight spot. Your first thought was not to find someone *else* to solve your problem. You had to think *yourself* out of a sticky situation.

What you went through might be seen as a full-blown emergency for a kid today, but you took it in stride.

Looking back on those BC days,

you were a free-wheeling, self-assured risk-taker and you didn't even know it.

Don't get me wrong—this is not to pooh-pooh technology. I'm as grateful as anyone for the Internet, my phone and the mash-ups my family can do on Skype. I've been fast friends with my mobile since the night my son mangled his leg on the lacrosse field at our local community center. Although I was right inside at a meeting, I was oblivious to his ordeal because no one outside knew I was there and I'd left my phone in the car. Thankfully, my husband was carrying his.

Still, as much as I like instant access to my loved ones and a world of information at my fingertips, I feel diminished. I worry that we humans are so bowled over by our Alt-brains of smartphones and Google and GPS, we're developing an inferiority complex.

We're disregarding our own amazing powers.

"No machine can do what they do."

The awesomeness of humans first struck me in Italy on a tour of a parmesan cheese factory. A red-haired, pony-tailed guide named Flavio was explaining how wizened experts determine exactly when the world-famous cheese is ready for market. Using full-body gestures, Flavio demonstrated how the inspectors painstakingly tap, sniff, and scratch each giant ochre wheel. Only when they are completely satisfied with what they hear, smell and feel will they stamp a cheese with their seal of approval.

Suddenly Flavio stopped and turned to us, uttering with reverence, "No machine can do what they do."

That's what I'm talking about.

Each of us is one of a kind— an absolute individual—packed with extraordinary resources, starting with our masterful palette of senses.

That would include the famous five plus all the others like intuition, humor and—especially in kids—the all-important sense of wonder. Then there's our curiosity, our capacity for conscience and compassion, and even our life-saving muscle memory.

Just think about how we analog people differ from digital devices. Tablets aren't like parents who just *know* when their toddler is about to throw a tantrum in the supermarket. Smartphones can't discern a fine Cabernet or enjoy a good laugh (and don't be fooled by Siri's funny lines—they're scripted by clever people). When confronted with the grandeur of Yosemite, computers have no breath to take away.

Only humans themselves, such as fragrance maestro Kilian Hennessy, understand how to conduct symphonies with our minds and senses. Although he descends from the famous cognac maker, Hennessy bottles stories.

> "I work like a director looking for a screenplay that will open the doors of the imagination." —Kilian Hennessy

In his concoctions, the French scent creator aims to capture passion, or "the intoxicating scent of a lover you nearly want to devour." To a laptop, pleasure does not compute.

Magic happens when humans touch.

If it were possible to bottle a hug, it could be sold as a combination muscle relaxant, tranquilizer and love potion. Our fingers are veritable magic wands. Behavioral research shows that when a loving adult pats a babbling baby at just the right moment, the baby's vocabulary is turbocharged. iPads aren't equipped to do that.

We perform astounding feats without even thinking about it.

On 9/11 inside World Trade Center Tower 2, intuition told Rick Rescorla, Morgan Stanley Dean Witter security chief, to ignore Port Authority orders for occupants to stay at their desks. Instead, Rescorla led more than 2,700 terrified co-workers down 44 flights to safety. The employees calmly followed as they had on his mandatory fire drills. The memory of those practice escapes, stored in their brainstems, moved their muscles even as their conscious minds seemed paralyzed by fear.

"The brainstem is like a bodyguard who's always watching your back, constantly scanning the environment for potential threats. The thinking brain is too slow for such an important task," explains behavioral therapist Dr. Suzanne LaCombe. "So for example, when a 90-mile-an-hour curve ball's coming at you, it's the reptilian brain that reflexively jerks your head out of the way before you even realize what's happening." That means you can move as fast as a gazelle spotting a lion on the Serengeti.

Our animality is something to celebrate, not ignore.

"For too long we've closed ourselves to the participatory life of our senses," says nature philosopher David Abram in *Becoming Animal*.

"We've taken our primary truths from technologies that hold the world at a distance." –David Abram

Getting in touch with your animal side is a pleasure, not a burden, since it usually involves going outside. There, we can get back in tune with nature's rhythms and sort out tangled thoughts. As naturalist and thinker Martin Ogle believes, "There are a lot of questions that being outdoors helps answer."

Richard Louv seconds that notion in his 2006 bestseller, *Last Child in the Woods*: "One might argue that the Internet has replaced the woods, in terms of inventive space, but no electronic environment stimulates all the senses."

But since we spend so much time with our Alt-brains, we don't get out much. Our very thoughts and actions are now moderated by the way we interact with our devices. Whereas people in the past grew up to think *differently*, more and more today we are thinking *the same*.

"What's happening is that we might, in fact, be at a time in our history where we're being domesticated by these great big societal things, such as Facebook and the Internet," says Mark Pagel, fellow of the Royal Society and professor of evolutionary biology. "We're being domesticated by them because fewer and fewer of us have to be innovators to get by."

To be "domesticated" is to become bland and similar—more like a herd of sheep.

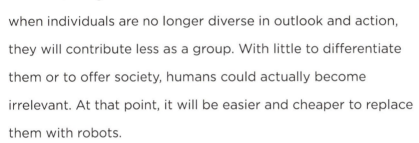

The danger is that when individuals are no longer diverse in outlook and action, they will contribute less as a group. With little to differentiate them or to offer society, humans could actually become irrelevant. At that point, it will be easier and cheaper to replace them with robots.

Chris Poole was 15 years old in 2003 when he founded image-sharing forum 4chan. Recently, he created a stir at the tech and music haven South by Southwest when he blasted two Internet titans. "Google and Facebook would have you believe that your online personality is a mirror of who you are," he claimed. "In fact it's more like a diamond; you show different facets of your personality to different people. Facebook has tried to force a fast-food industry approach to identity." To Poole, "Identity is prismatic."

So to survive in a world of tireless, mass-produced gadgets

we humans—like diamonds—must be durable.

According to Merriam-Webster, durable means "able to exist for a long time without significant deterioration." Or, as the slogan goes: "Built to Last."

Over the millennia, we humans have grown ever more durable by using our minds and senses to solve problems. We not only rolled with life's punches, we also learned from them and moved forward.

But now that we rely so much on smart gadgets, our sharp human edge is getting duller. After eons of advancements, our species may have begun to *devolve*.

Yet our degradation is not inevitable. If we put our minds to it, we can put the shine back on the human apple. We can stop our slide toward sameness if we stand up and cheer,

Hooray for humans!

As world-renowned biologist E.O. Wilson tells us, it's a matter of survival: "The more we ignore our health and welfare, the greater are the many threats to our own species."

My hope is that if society values what it means to be durable, human-only skills will be designed *in* to jobs rather than designed *out*.

Being durable may certainly help the species, but what will it do for you?

You'll worry less, sleep better and feel less overwhelmed.

Because you'll be more in control of your time, you can rekindle genuine relationships with the people you love. With new energy to tackle the day, you'll ignite your inner genius, have more light bulb moments and give off a "Hire me!" aura that will attract potential employers. Plus, you'll rely more on yourself and be better prepared for life's curve balls and emergencies.

The big bonus is that once you're more durable, you'll be prepared to raise **creative, more durable kids.**

If you are a parent, being durable will set you apart from your peers who will still be confused and concerned about when and how to introduce their children to technology. You'll have perspective on books with titles like *Born Digital* which suggest that human nature has somehow changed and babies now arrive knowing how to code. You'll understand that today's newborns are just like those who came before them— they're as wild and untethered as the squirrels in the trees.

Only later will a child plug in to the digital world, and you'll have everything to do with when that happens.

Until then, early childhood is the only time in life when a person is completely free to discover his or her native "gifts." I'm not saying that gifts of tablets and apps are not amazing, but their time will come. In the meantime, when toddlers range around, freely using all of their senses to examine, taste and play with whatever they choose, they are making rich and lifelong neural connections.

Indeed, when children are able to naturally explore their world, they are creating sense-memories they can return to as adults for solace and inspiration.

If you grew up without a cell phone, consider yourself lucky.

For all your unplugged, BC years you relied largely on your own judgment and you had wild time to develop genuine relationships with others and to uncover your own unique talents and quirks.

Today, though, the pressure is intense to close a child's wild human window.

The problem is that if kids spend too much time with technology too soon, they may never fully establish their own operating systems and understand what makes *themselves* tick.

Because toddlers are so quick with a touch screen, parents might mistake that as a sign of intelligence. But the reality is that consumer gadgets are designed to be no-brainers. "It's like learning to use toothpaste," says Alan Eagle, a speechwriter for top tech executives. "At Google and all these places we make technology as brain-dead easy to use as possible."

Other parents worry their children will fall behind if not introduced to technology as soon as possible. But the fact is that once a child plugs in, wild humanhood is over. Looking ahead, if kids' interests and skills are unrealized or too similar, society and innovation will surely suffer.

Today's parents' sacred trust is to *jealously guard their children's chance to be wild;* **to give them time, not to take it away.**

Even when the time does come for a child to enter the digital world, the sacred trust still applies. So that kids are durable for a lifetime, they need to continue mining their inner gifts and to be in touch with the natural world around them.

But who is a "durable human"?

We can learn a lot from the true story of four-year-old Alex and his 23-year-old mom. One day not long ago, Alex was playing in the basement of their townhouse when he heard a loud *thud*. Bolting toward the sound, he found his mom lying at the bottom of the stairs. He pushed her and yelled in her ear, but she wouldn't move.

Thinking for a second, he ran for her cellphone, unlocked the keyboard, and pressed three numbers. When a lady answered and asked his address, he promptly answered.

"I can't understand you," she told him. "You're gonna have to tell me again." After repeating himself almost to the point of tears, she *finally* got it. The reason the dispatcher had trouble understanding Alex is because he was *singing*. Only a few weeks before, Alex's mom took the time to teach him their address in the form of a little tune. She taught him to dial 911 when he first started playing with her phone. Months after her accident, she stood by proudly as the mayor gave Alex the Kid Hero award, glad to see how her simple lessons paid off for both of them.

Alex and his mom are *durable humans*. They *fully engage* their brains, each other, and—when they need to—the tools at hand.

So, what's the secret sauce for durability?
Turns out, the recipe is simple.

First, know how to do stuff.

It's important to have skills so you can do things for yourself.

Second, maintain genuine relationships with other people,

which tends to work best when we're in the same place at the same time. If Alex's mom hadn't sat down and patiently taught him one-on-one, he wouldn't have known how to save her.

Third, take time to follow your curiosity.

That may mean spending time alone, where your wild ideas can bubble to the surface. As Anne Morrow Lindbergh writes in *Gift from the Sea*, in solitude we can "plant our own dream blossoms."

Parents also need to help their children follow their hearts. Dave Grohl plops down on the floor with his kids and plays old records on a turntable. By exposing his daughters to different types of music, he hopes each will connect with her own unique essence. As he told the throngs at South by Southwest, whatever you do—"whether you incite a riot or a revolution"—the important thing is to find your own voice.

The Hawaiian word *maka'ala* means to be fully alert and present. In the same way, being durable is to be mindful of yourself and your circumstances.

To jumpstart your creativity, you may need to take a break from the task at hand to "open your sense doors," in the words of *wisdom 2.0* author, Soren Gordhamer.

Sometimes, it's when we're forced from the familiar that our durability will shine. Just ask anyone who had to contend with the likes of Sandy or Katrina.

Where do you begin *your own path* toward Durable?

Remember Flavio's message: humans can do things that machines can't. Consider what you've already done today—when have you shown curiosity, creativity, compassion or heart?

Maybe you noticed your dog was limping and you took her to the vet. Or you whipped up a delectable omelet for breakfast. Perhaps you rode your bike to the store instead of driving. Why is that durable? When you are self-propelled you are self-reliant, plus you get a taste of the freedom you had as a kid jetting around on your banana seat.

So, it's not so hard to be durable. Sometimes it just comes naturally.

Why did I write this Manifesto?

This book is a love letter to my three wonderful kids—and in honor of all grownup, present and future children—a reminder that they each have a one-of-a-kind essence to cherish and protect. I want them to take to heart the message of beloved children's TV host Mr. Rogers, immortalized in the PBS Digital Studios remix, "Garden of Your Mind":

"It's good to be curious about many things. **You can think about things and make believe. All you have to do is** *think and they'll grow."*
—Fred Rogers

Please visit DurableHuman.com
to share your thoughts and ideas

Made in the USA
Lexington, KY
04 September 2014